Walking in the winter

by Beverley Randell

In **winter**, the days are short.
It is dark in the morning.
We get up in the dark,
and it is dark again by bedtime.

Winter is a cold time,
and we put on warm things.

If you go
for a walk
in winter,
look at the trees.
Some trees still
have green leaves.
They are
evergreen trees.

Some trees have
old brown leaves,
or no leaves at all,
in winter.
They are
deciduous trees.

Everything outside
gets cold in winter.
Water gets cold at night.
Very cold water
turns into **ice**.
Winter is the time
for ice and snow.

If the winter is very cold,
birds get hungry.

We can
give them food.
Some birds like
bread and birdseed,
and some like fat.

Some birds
will eat
fruit
and nuts.

In winter,
some little animals **hibernate**.

They go to sleep
for a long time.

Frogs hide in the mud
and hibernate.

In winter, hedgehogs hibernate in nests made of leaves.

Snails hibernate, too.
They stay inside their shells and don't come out.

Bears hibernate in winter,
but most big animals do not.
Deer do not hibernate.

A fox made
this set of tracks
in the snow.
It was out looking
for food.

13

Summer is the time
for flowers,
but some trees
have flowers
in **winter**!

This tree has
yellow flowers.

This tree has
red flowers
in winter.

At the end of winter,
the days get longer.
The first spring flowers come out,
and we can see
that **spring** is coming.